WILD ABOUT YOU
Friends With Feathers

By Peta Boyce and Lyn Ellison

Friends With Feathers

A collection of stories
about birds who accepted
a helping hand and gave
something back in return

Illustrated and written by
wildlife artists
Peta Boyce & Lyn Ellison

For our *real* children
Josh and Ryan
Kelly and Merryon

Other books by Lyn Ellison
'Wild About You - Lucky Chance'

Published by Magpie Art Prints,
2 Braeside Cres., Maudsland Q'ld., 4210, Australia
First Published 2000
Illustrations and text Copyright Peta Boyce and Lyn Ellison
Printed by Toppan, Hong Kong
Design and layout by Peta Boyce and Lyn Ellison

National Library of Australia Cataloguing-in-Publication Data
Boyce, Peta, 1957-
Friends with feathers.
ISBN 0 9585878 2 5
1.Birds - Australia. 2. Wildlife rescue - Australia.
3. Wildlife rehabilitation - Australia. I .Ellison, Lyn, 1943-
II. Title. (Series:Wild About You)
639.9780994

Contents

Looking for Mum - White-breasted Woodswallows

Introduction

It was back in May 1998 that the concept for "Wild About You" was conceived. Lyn and I were working together for the first time preparing our joint exhibition, "Feathers and Fur". Lyn was raising a wallaroo, ' Lucky' and during the final days of preparation for the exhibition we began swapping anecdotes about some of the animals, past and present, we had cared for. Lyn suggested I write a book about my experiences and my immediate answer was "I've thought about it, but it sounds like one big headache." Lyn replied with "Oh no, not at all, it would be fun!" Well, it's been both. I'm sure neither of us realized at the time the huge task we were about to undertake, nor the personal satisfaction we would have.

Lyn was very keen to tell Lucky's story (Wild About You - Lucky Chance) and we both decided to work together on a separate book devoted entirely to birds. Neither book was intended to be a guide about caring for wildlife, but rather a collection of stories, sometimes poignant, sometimes humorous, about our wonderful and unique native fauna and how they affected our lives whilst living in our homes.

The birds depicted in the stories are all real birds, with personalities as diverse as their specific needs. From the diminutive Styles, who touched my life like no other, to the bold and brash drongo and Lyn's delightful Maggie, they were all truly wonderful individuals. By telling their stories we hope to create more awareness of Australian wildlife, in particular our marvellous birds. You will learn that a "drongo" isn't necessarily a colloquial name for a fool but a bright, intelligent native bird and that not all magpies want to attack people in spring but can be warm, friendly and extremely playful.

The paintings have been included to enhance the text and also to assist the reader in recognizing some of the different species. Most of the paintings depict the birds either in the wild or in a garden setting where many of them can be found.

We have both had some wonderful experiences caring for wildlife and although there has been heartache, the trust and friendship displayed by some of these individuals makes it all worth while - our *friends with feathers.*

Peta Boyce

Cuddles & Co.- Silvereyes

Styles

"What on earth is that!"

My older son, Josh was staring in amazement at me feeding a tiny, funny looking little bird who was sporting a spiky, grey green mohawk hairstyle.

"Check the style" was his next remark and "Styles", the baby silvereye was named.

Styles had been found the previous day fluttering helplessly on a busy footpath. An early morning walker had very nearly stepped on the tiny creature, not much bigger than a bumble-bee and taken Styles to one of the local vets. When I received him later in the day he appeared to be in good health and was begging vigorously to be fed.

Styles was the first small bird to come into my care and my first reaction was he was far too small for me to raise. However, with the help of Jane, a fellow carer and good friend, I was able to overcome my initial misgivings in my ability and found the little bird to be no trouble at all, just small.

Some carers are reluctant to raise many of our smaller birds because of their diminutive size. There is the illusion of these birds being more fragile than some of the larger species, but that is all it is, an illusion. Over the years I've found these little birds to be quite hardy, and the success rate is quite high if their few special needs are met. They do require more constant feeding and due to their faster metabolism, it is important to get their diet right fairly quickly. For the carer, it is an advantage to have good eyesight and a steady hand for getting food into tiny mouths.

Styles was certainly no problem to feed. He'd sit up in his artificial nest, head shaking, beak wide open yelling his head off. I used a toothpick to feed him and we often joked about Styles having a toothpick for a mother. Once he was full he'd tip his little bottom over the edge of the nest for me to catch and remove his single dropping, snuggle down, close his eyes and off to sleep. After half an hour or so we repeated the procedure.

Within two days Styles was perching on the edge of his nest. I was amazed at how quickly he had grown in such a short time. His flight feathers had shed their quills, he had a stumpy little tail and his mohawk had become thicker. He was still completely bald from the edge of his beak, around his eyes and back to his ear openings, giving him a faintly comical appearance. Later research revealed that although silvereyes live in flocks, they become extremely territorial  during the breeding season. To prevent their parents mistaking them for another adult and driving them away, young silvereyes don't attain the characteristic white feathers around their eyes until they are nearly independent.

On day three I got the shock of my life, although I think Styles may have got a bigger one. He flew straight off the edge of the nest and disappeared inside my open handbag. A typical handbag! Full of everything except the proverbial kitchen sink! He still wasn't much bigger than a bumble-bee. How was I going to get him out without squashing him? How was I even going to find him in there, the bag from hell! As I stood there in horror trying to work out what to do , a shaken little bird appeared, blinked at me and uttered a quiet little peep. First flights can certainly be a bit hazardous.

When Styles came to me I was still relatively inexperienced and wildlife care was not as organised as it is today. There were a few carers scattered around the area, however there was no organisation to call for help or to match up birds, to get species "flocked up". By raising species in groups it helps to prevent "imprinting" and as the babies mature they usually become quite wild, making them far better prospects for release. Styles never got that chance.

Attempts were made to get Styles ready for release. After he had been in a large cage for a couple of weeks and was feeding himself, his cage was put outside with some of the other birds. He looked even smaller against his rainbow lorikeet neighbours. I was met the next morning by his cage hanging askew off the wall and a frightened little bird huddled in the corner. One wing was slightly injured and there was blood on his face, possibly from trying to push it through the wire. I was sure a marauding cat was the culprit although none of the other birds had been touched.

Once again his cage was brought back into the house. He recovered quickly from his injuries and a couple of days later I put his cage back outside. This time I decided to bring him back inside at night and for a while this arrangement appeared to work well. Little birds love a bit of sunshine and frequently sunbathe and Styles would sit there on his perch, wings and tail fanned out, eyes closed, head tilted, relishing the sun's warmth. Then the magpies found him.

Fortunately I was home at the time. I heard the magpies warbling, then the lorikeets started up their racket. Something was amiss. When I went outside to investigate there were two juvenile magpies sitting on top of Styles' cage and an adult hanging off the side, all after an easy meal. The stricken silvereye was flying frantically back and forth in his cage trying desperately to escape. The magpies flew off as soon as I appeared and Styles collapsed exhausted. This time he had nearly lost his eye. Back into the house he came. It was definitely not safe outside for little birds unless supervised.

I did make one more attempt at a release. It didn't seem fair to keep him, he was a wild bird and the aim of wildlife care is to eventually be able to release the animals. Silvereyes used to frequent our garden and Styles regularly answered their calls. Early one morning, when a flock was feeding amongst the flowers of a bottlebrush, I put Styles' cage outside and opened the door. He panicked. He flew out of the cage and fluttered into a shrub. In his fright he shrieked an alarm call, scattering the wild birds. He appeared confused, flying only short distances before fluttering to the ground or crashing into a shrub. Eventually he landed on the wire of one of the aviaries. He was panting heavily and obviously quite distressed. Disappointed, I picked him up and put him back into his cage. Only on two other occasions was Styles ever out of his cage and both times his behaviour was the same. In fact, over the years these were the only times he was ever truly terrified of anything.

It appeared Styles was here for the long haul. I had contacted the Wildlife Ranger for our area and after explaining the situation I was issued a permit to keep him indefinitely. In the meantime I had called other carers, trying to get another silvereye, but the outlook didn't seem promising. Nobody had silvereyes and it was three years before another one came into care. By then Styles had become hopelessly imprinted. He was without fear, friendly towards humans; he did not even live outside. If released he would not have lasted five minutes.

Little did I know at the time the huge impact this diminutive bundle of feathers would make, not only on my life, but the whole family. Maybe it was because he was so small and small can become insignificant. Not Styles. He was a big bird in a little body.

The interest Styles would create with first time visitors was always amusing. They would be thoroughly entertained by the lorikeets, commenting on their beautiful colours, laughing at their tricks. They would admire the arrogant Eric, the Indian Ringneck, who would say "hello" if he was in a good mood. Then they would glance at Styles and begin to walk away. Quickly I would introduce them "This is Styles, he likes a scratch", put my hand into his cage, he'd hop over, fluff his feathers and allow me to scratch his head. All of a sudden the visitor would become interested, "What sort of bird is he?", "Is he a finch?", "What does he eat?", "How did you get him?", "Where can I buy one?" We have interstate friends who always asked after Styles before any other animal.

Because it wasn't safe to put Styles outside unattended, we moved his cage around the house to wherever he could get the sun. Through the winter months his cage was kept in the lounge room, as part of the family. I can't recall exactly when his bad eating habits began but I clearly remember the day when Ryan, a pre-schooler at the time, was lying on the floor watching television, eating a jam sandwich. I watched as Ryan, eyes still glued to the television, held his sandwich out to share with Styles. Ryan would take a bite, pass it back to Styles, Styles would take a bite, not once did Ryan avert his eyes from the screen. From then on whatever we were eating we were expected to share. Styles would fly onto the side of the cage, poke his face through the wire to see what we had, call softly to us and if nothing was forthcoming he would start demanding with a loud "pweee", a sound similar to his alarm call. Red cordial iceblocks were by far his favourite and he would yell at the children, even if they were on the other side of the room.

Birds in the wild spend a large part of their day foraging for food. To alleviate boredom and break the monotony of their day I try to offer my birds a wide variety of food, suitable to their diets. "Don't you get sick of feeding all those animals?" is a question I am often asked, "Not really," I answer, "Feeding time is the fun time." I enjoy it when they greet you as you arrive

Striated Pardalotes

with their dishes and it's a pleasure to watch them sorting through what's on the menu, looking for their favourite titbits. Styles was especially appreciative, twittering softly to me as I put fresh food in his cage each morning. He would fly to his dishes and have a quick taste of everything before settling back to the "best bits" first. He always had at least three different types of soft fruit to choose from. As grapes were his favourite I bought them year round, even through the winter months paying exorbitant prices. "Don't eat the grapes, they're for Styles" was as familiar to my children as "Clean your teeth." Strangely, Styles was never particularly fond of cherries and yet silvereyes can do a vast amount of damage in the cherry orchards.

Silvereyes in the wild eat a variety of small insects and although Styles was offered mealworms each day we still caught as many "bugs" for him as we could find. He was particularly fond of aphids and would spend hours carefully picking them off any branches I put into his cage. Scale insects, small caterpillars, mosquitos and March flies were all eaten with gusto. Small spiders were a particular favourite, Styles becoming quite excited when he saw us walking towards his cage carrying one dangling from its web. What wonderful small birds to encourage into your garden.

Many gardeners and birdwatchers tend to dismiss the silvereye. They're common, small, quite plain, nothing really outstanding about them at all. But pause one day and listen to a cock silvereye in full song. Not a loud song, but the notes are as clear as any canary's. When Styles sang I would often take a pause from whatever I was doing just to listen to him. I often heard my husband Denis say, "Thank you Styles, that was nice", as though it was expected of him.

For some strange reason Styles developed an abiding hatred of feet. Feet on the floor were fine, feet propped up were another matter. Nobody could lie on the lounge with their feet near his cage. As soon as "the feet" left the floor he would be onto the wire, beak clacking, wings down, screaming his

alarm call. For a small bird the silvereye alarm is extremely loud and it goes on and on and on. Eventually the offending feet would have to be put back on the floor, usually after someone had shouted "Shut up, we can't hear the T.V." Sometimes Styles' cage would be put in our bedroom, facing the foot of the bed. Denis likes to kick his feet out from under the covers and there was nothing quite like being woken at daybreak by a dreadful, shrieking racket that would begin as soon as it was light enough for Styles to see feet. We used to joke that maybe it was because he was nearly stepped on when he was a baby.

Along with Styles' foot fetish he also developed a dislike for small children. This is not uncommon and I wonder if it's the quick movements and higher pitch of their voices that birds find disconcerting. Little kids love to poke their fingers through the wire of cages and as we have a few parrots this can mean a nasty nip to a small finger. Styles was a great help in this respect. Many children, even though you warn them that the bird will bite, still insist on poking their fingers into a cage. Styles was particularly tempting as he was so small and cute. "Don't poke your fingers in the cage, Styles will bite you." The child would look at me as if I had rocks in my head and promptly poke his or her finger into the cage. Styles would immediately dart across, beak clacking and peck them sharply. His small beak never really hurt them but they would get a fright and most never poked their fingers into any of the cages after that.

Two of Josh's teenage friends also received the wrath of Styles. He had known Ben for quite a few years when suddenly he decided that he really wasn't too keen on "that boy".   Poor Ben, he had never done anything to harm him , Styles had just decided. As soon as Ben walked near his cage Styles would drop his wings and begin beak clacking. He did eventually get over it when Ben housesat for us and was feeding him. Matthew was a different matter. Maybe it was the deep tone of his voice, we don't really know, but we nearly went crazy. As soon as the boy spoke Styles would set up a racket, the same alarm used for the feet. Many times when Matthew knocked on the door he was greeted with "Sssh, don't speak."

For most of the year Styles was happy enough living in his half way world between human and bird. We had become his surrogate flock, he shared our food, he could elicit preening behaviour from us by coming to the edge of his cage and raising his feathers and he had a pom pom to snuggle into. However, during the breeding season he became irritable and began to exhibit territorial behaviour.

I had given him a little cane basket nest to busy himself with when he began making nest building signs. He would spend hours tearing strips of paper from the floor of his cage and poking the pieces into the gaps in the cane. He would then perch on the side of his nest, wings down, fluttering rapidly, lower his head down into the nest and call softly. However, if we walked too near the cage he would fly onto the wire, beak clacking in anger, to drive us away. Sometimes at night during this time of the year he would call as though to other birds. I then read where silvereyes often migrate after dark and obviously he could hear these birds and was returning their calls. My heart went out to him at these times, his frustration at not fulfilling his role in life became my frustration. I vowed to do anything to prevent this happening again.

About a year after Styles came to me, the wildlife organisation, Wilvos was formed. I became a member and the word was spread around that I had a silvereye. It was still another two years before two babies came into care and were sent to me. By now it was too late to release Styles, but with these two new babies, I took a gamble that paid off and gave Styles a role to play during the breeding season.

After a few days in quarantine, to make sure the babies were strong and healthy, I put them in their artificial nest into Styles' cage. At this stage I was unsure how Styles would react; would he be frightened, or worse attack the babies and injure them? Styles flew down to the nest and perched on the side, head cocked sideways. He reached over and pulled gently at one of the nestlings, looked at me as if to say "What's this, it isn't food?" then flew off and ignored them. However, it was the reaction of the babies that encouraged me. They were very interested in Styles - they begged to him and watched him flying and eating. Although I still had to feed them, Styles "fostered" the babies. Over the following years Styles helped raise approximately twenty baby silvereyes.

The babies would fledge more quickly and from watching Styles eat they became independent from me sooner and they all went wild. As long as Styles had "foster children" the territorial behaviour ceased. It was wonderful to watch the younger birds snuggle into him and preen him. However, once the babies began to show signs of maturity - the white feathers around the eyes - Styles would become aggressive towards them, a sign to me that they were now ready to be released.

Styles had lived nearly all his life in our home with two cats regularly passing by his cage. They ignored him and he never seemed to take any notice of them. I was completely stunned and am still fascinated by what happened next. Styles had two youngsters with him in the cage and all three were down feeding, about a foot above floor level, when one of the cats walked past. Styles screamed the alarm call and flew to the top of the cage with the babies following. The cat had not done a thing, not even so much as a sideways glance and I couldn't understand the reaction. However, this became a regular occurrence; if the birds were down low near the cat, Styles would sound the alarm and move higher. When Styles was on his own however, he didn't take any notice of the cats. Was he teaching the young birds about predators? I wonder.

Styles had learnt that when he was in the house he was quite safe and I watched in amusement one day when a butcherbird, the scourge of silvereyes, landed on the window ledge near his cage. Poor Styles nearly fell off his perch in fright, then in an attempt to save face he dropped his wings, beak clacked and screamed abuse at the other bird. Eventually the butcherbird flew off, Styles watching him go, continuing to yell at him until he was out of sight.

I was awakened in the early hours one morning by the sound of the birds flapping in the studio. Maybe Eric had fallen off his perch again, I wondered, reluctant to get out of bed. Then I heard distress cries from the silvereyes. Now I was forced to move and as I got up Denis stirred and mumbling asked me what was the problem. "It's O.K., I'm just checking on the birds" I answered as he drifted back to sleep.

We have a few large geckos living in the house and as I made my way into the studio I thought that maybe one of them had run across a cage and frightened the birds. Only the previous day I had removed from Styles' cage three young silvereyes to be released. There were also four pardalotes and a brown honeyeater in the room, all of them making a racket. "What on earth is going on" I thought as I switched on the light. I couldn't believe my eyes and reeled back in shock. There in the young silvereyes' cage was a brown tree snake coiled around one of the babies, *my* babies. The bird was already dead and the other two were frantically flying around the cage.

It took a moment for me to gather myself together enough to call "Denis, I think you'd better get up, we've got a problem." I was still staring at the cage in disbelief trying to comprehend the scene before me when Denis appeared at the door. "A snake has got one of the silvereyes" I said, still unable to look away from the horror. "What do you want me do?" he asked.
It was then that I looked at my husband swaying on his feet, still groggy from sleep, blinking in the bright light, wearing a T-Shirt and nothing else. I glanced back at the snake, now starting to eat the bird, looked back at my half asleep, half naked husband and thinking I must be going mad, said "I think you'd better put some pants on."

We did eventually remove the snake from the cage and relocate him and I can't deny that I was really angry about what had happened. The cheek of the thing coming into my home and eating one of my babies. What did concern us though was that we couldn't find where the snake had got in and for weeks afterwards every sound through the night had me running into the studio to check on the birds. Also, I couldn't bear to think about how I would have reacted if it had been Styles and how fortunate he was that it had not been him.

The weekend was not beginning on a good note. The morning had begun with a phone call from Georgetown, a small town in far north Queensland. All week I had been helping a carer, Annette, from this isolated town, with an injured boobook owl. Numerous phone calls had been made relaying advice from our local vet and a raptor expert. It had been a wonderful story of hope for one small bird as the Georgetown community had rallied to assist. Patrons at the local pub had caught crickets and grasshoppers to help feed the owl, and as there is no vet in the town the boobook had been seen by the flying doctor when he arrived on his weekly visit. Sadly, despite all our efforts, Annette had rung to tell me the owl had died that morning.

At times like this it is so easy to become disillusioned with wildlife care and I was feeling very depressed and despondent as I started the birds' morning feeds. When I got to Styles' cage I felt as though I had been struck. Styles was sitting tightly on his perch, fluffed up with his head tucked under his wing. He showed little interest in his food when it was put into his cage, an

Brown Honeyeater

Bottlebrush Breakfast - Silvereyes

obvious sign he was very ill. *Oh no, please not Styles. Why Styles?* I cried to myself.

I gently picked him up to feel him over and found a large lump above his thigh, on his abdomen. My chest constricted and I felt as though I couldn't breathe. From years of experience working with these small birds I knew that once one became as ill as this there was very little chance of recovery. I mixed a broad spectrum antibiotic into his nectar and although I had little faith in it working, I had to feel as though I was doing something.

Later that day I moved Styles' cage into our bedroom, where it was quieter and put the heat lamp on to help keep him more comfortable. I decided not to put him in a "hospital cage" as I felt he would only become more stressed by moving him into something unfamiliar. Throughout the night I would get up to check on him and help him get back up to his favourite perch as he had become weak very quickly. Each time I picked him up he would twitter softly to me as though he was saying thank you. He appeared confused by his condition and I felt overwhelmingly helpless.

Sunday continued much the same although there were moments when I felt sure there had been a slight improvement. However, Sunday night when I checked him over I couldn't believe how much weight he had lost in such a short time. Styles died later the next afternoon.

In the eight years that Styles lived in our home I developed an ongoing passion for our smaller birds. Often I sat near him watching as he bathed, preening his feathers, listening to his beautiful song. He provided inspiration for many paintings of small birds. It was always so hard to believe that so much intelligence and personality could fit in such a small body.

The aim of caring for wildlife is to rehabilitate and release our native fauna back into their own wild world. Unfortunately Styles was a victim of circumstance and although he remained in my care, he was never viewed as a pet. I have continued to 'take-in' silvereyes and recently successfully raised and released another three, all as wild as can be. When the first nestling arrived after Styles, Denis looked at me "Another Styles?" he queried. We answered the question simultaneously, "No, there will never be another Styles."

Dad's Home - Red-backed Wrens

Living With Fairies

It was with a sense of irritation that I answered the phone that morning. I was trying to finish a commissioned painting and often when I'm working I ignore any phone calls. "Peta, it's Paul from the school. Sorry to disturb you but I've got a nest here with three tiny baby birds. I think they might be wrens."

Wrens! My mood instantly changed. They are a favourite subject of mine to paint and for a long time I had yearned to raise them, to get "up close and personal". For years I had been remarking to other carers that we never get orphaned wrens and only rarely an injured adult. These are a common bird in our area and due to their habit of nesting on or near the ground, close to human habitation it was strange that they did not come into care.

I could barely contain my excitement and did not hesitate to ask Paul if he could bring the birds straight round. So much for a morning's work. Little did I know it would be another two weeks before I would pick up a paint brush again.

When Paul arrived he gave me the full story of a very lucky escape for these tiny creatures. The local school has an ongoing rainforest replanting project and as the initial stage is now about ten years old it is lush enough to supply a host of small birds with somewhere to live. Surrounding the rainforest are open paddocks with long grass - suitable habitat for red-backed wrens. Paul and his off-sider, Jim, had been brush-cutting the long grass at the edge of the rainforest and from around the bottom of some shrubs. Paul was called away for a period of time, leaving the clearing to his helper. When he returned, Jim informed him he had knocked a nest out from under a shrub. It was amazing that the nest was still completely intact. Anyway, he had put the nest back and had shown Paul the "parents" sitting "up there in that tree." Paul looked up at two butcherbirds who were already eyeing off an easy meal. He knew that with the nest now completely exposed it would be too dangerous for the adult wrens to return and if it was left there the babies

would be eaten.

Red-backed wrens are the smallest of the fairy wrens and I peered into the nest at three of the tiniest baby birds I had ever seen. The nestlings were still blind and naked, although there was the beginning of the dark lines on their bodies indicating that pin feathers were not far from emerging. When I gently blew through the side opening of the nest - mimicking the arrival of an adult to feed them - the babies all began begging vigorously. This is always an encouraging sign, in particular with smaller birds. If they beg for too long without being fed they become exhausted, they stop begging and it is almost impossible to feed them.

Because the side opening of the nest was so small I had to cut the top away to make it easier to feed them. Usually I remove baby birds from their existing nest and put them into an artificial one lined with tissues as it is easier to keep clean. However, the three wrens were so small and packed so tightly into their bed of soft grasses that I was worried about injuring them if I tried to take them out. I decided to leave them where they were for the time being and hoped the nest would stay healthy.

I was able to feed a small mealworm to each of the babies and as soon as they had eaten they flipped their little bottoms over and deposited a neat little white sac on the rim of the nest for me to remove. Then they snuggled down and went to sleep. O.K., I thought to myself, this is going to be easy.

The first day I fed the babies every half hour; small mealworms, minute strips of ox-heart and tiny pieces of low-fat cheese. Their droppings stayed in a neat package indicating that the change in diet hadn't upset their tummies. I was then able to remove the sac without rupturing it and spilling the contents into the nest. This may all sound very easy but in actual fact it was quite a strain as everything was so small. Tiny gapes, minute portions of food, all done with a pair of tweezers and a steady hand. By the end of the first day I was exhausted and thought I was going to go blind from straining my eyes.

Day two and the babies were feeding well so I extended their meal times to every hour. With other small birds, when they are left a little bit longer between feeds they soon adjust to eating more in one sitting, filling up. Not the wrens. They would take two or three pieces and go back to sleep. I would blow on the nest, jiggle the nest, tap on the side of it, anything to wake them up. And if I was very lucky they would reluctantly open their beaks and take just one more piece. By the end of the day their droppings were diminishing in size; a sign they weren't getting enough to eat. "Oh well", I thought, "I'll put them back on half hourly feeds for a day or two and by then they should be a bit bigger and go longer." If only I knew how wrong I would be.

Their feeding habits were not at all like pardalotes, another species of little insectivorous bird I had raised. I wondered if it was because fairy wrens live in family groups, older siblings helping to feed the younger ones, therefore ensuring a constant supply of food to the nest. However, baby pardalotes are fed only by their parents and at times would have to wait a while for their food, filling themselves when it was their turn.

The three little wrens had no intention of breaking the constant feeding habit. It didn't matter how hard I tried to extend their mealtimes they refused to take extra; two or three mouthfuls, no more. However, I have never seen baby birds grow so quickly. By the end of the first week their eyes had opened and they were clothed in soft brown feathers. And they were very, very cute.

Fortunately, into the second week I could feed them hourly. I was well and truly housebound and had only left the house once in the two weeks for a very quick grocery shop. I was reluctant to change their routine too much as they were all doing so well. After making enquiries I had not been able to find any other carers who had raised wrens, so I was really in the dark about their requirements.

Halfway through the third week they fledged (left the nest). This is always a major milestone as not long after fledging most baby birds begin to feed themselves, giving you a bit of a life back. Time for me to get back to work and get that painting finished.

The three would sit on their perch, snuggled tightly together throughout the day. Occasionally whoever was in the middle would stand and stretch his wings. The other two would quickly close the gap between them, their standing brother then being forced to scramble across their backs to get back onto the perch and snuggle down again. It was a delight to have them near me in the studio while I worked.

However, the beginning of the fourth week was a different story. For a few days before baby birds learn how to feed themselves they go through a stage of demanding food almost constantly; in fact every time they see their "parent". Other small birds will give you a bit of respite though and when they are in the studio with me will wait at least three quarters of an hour before a movement from me (like putting the paint brush in the paint) will send them into a frenzy, begging incessantly.

Not the wrens, they demanded constantly. By now they were flying around in a large cage which sat on a table behind where I worked. I would feed them and no sooner had I turned around and picked up the brush they would be begging again. I also had a couple of baby silvereyes at the time and when they heard the wrens begging they would start as well. Even the most patient of people will begin to feel irritated and after three days of this behaviour I felt like I was going to go nuts!

At this stage they were being fed a special mix, of which low-fat mince is the main ingredient, plus their mealworms. These items were now in the cage with them and they would hop across to their dishes, begging for me to pick up the food and feed it to them. In desperation I put towels over their cage so they could no longer see me, hoping this would force them to pick up the food themselves. I fed them and turned around to get back to work. All was quiet for fifteen minutes or so and those few moments were sheer bliss. I could hear their little feet tap, tapping on the paper on the floor of their cage and soft murmurings as they chattered away to each other. I now know they were hatching out a new plan of attack as the begging racket started again. I ignored them for as long as I could stand it. Finally I spun

Kidstuff - Red-backed Wrens

around angrily to be met by three little faces peering at me through a gap in the towels; all jostling frantically to get the best look at Mum. My irritation dissolved in an instant. Fortunately, the next day they started picking up their own food and I only needed to "top them up" in the morning and late afternoon.

The bond between these three little birds was extremely close, closer than I had ever noticed between other small birds. I don't recall ever seeing them bicker amongst themselves and yet there was a distinct pecking order. There was enough variation between the three that we referred to them as "Big", "Small" and "Fluffy". Big was the brave one; the decision maker and adventurer. On the odd occasion, in his excitement at being fed, Big had hopped out the door of his cage. He never panicked and would hop around confidently checking out his surroundings. Eventually the calls from his siblings would bring him back to the cage and I would pick him up and pop him back in. I had a rare treat one day when this tiny creature hopped onto my knee and stood there looking at me, head cocked sideways as though he was asking "Are you my Mother?" The trust displayed by this tiny bird, not much bigger than a butterfly, was truly humbling. It is a memory I will always treasure.

The day Fluffy snuck out the door was a different matter. He called back frantically to his siblings and each time I stooped to pick him up he would fly to another part of the room. Eventually, thanks to the other two birds returning his calls, Fluffy flew back to collapse exhausted on the top of the cage. It was a simple matter then to pick him up and put him back with the other two.

Not long after I had stopped hand feeding the wrens they began to become more timid and wild. They suffered badly with "night fright" and the studio had to be off limits after dark as I was concerned one of them would become seriously injured. As it was, Fluffy had bruised his hock and was slightly lame. I had been catching as many small insects as I could find and they were constantly foraging amongst the leaves of the branches in their cage. It had been six weeks since the wrens had come into care and although the first three weeks had been so intense, I found it hard to believe they were ready to go so soon. So quickly had Big changed from the trusting little creature sitting on my knee to one flying frantically around in the cage each time I had to put food in - desperate to get away. It was time for the wrens to be released.

Research has revealed that the red-backed wren is the most nomadic of the fairy wrens, establishing a temporary territory during the breeding season. Although the wrens had come from the school grounds the area was too open and did not provide enough shelter for it to be a safe release site. I had found what I hoped would be a suitable site, lots of tall trees with reasonably dense undergrowth and lots of blady grass growing in the more open areas. The site was part of a state forest area so the risk of human interference and attack by domestic pets was reduced. These little birds have enough to contend with in relation to native predators without these other added pressures. I frequently walked along the tracks through there and although I hadn't seen red-backed wrens I had often heard their calls.

A couple of hours after daybreak I put the wrens' cage into the car. I had my camera with me in anticipation of some good shots of their release. I always like to leave birds for release in their cages at the site (under my supervision) for a period of time as this helps to relax them. It gives them a chance to have a good look around at their new surroundings from the security and safety of their cage. This can be quite a frightening time for young birds with all the strange sights and sounds. It is not a good release if they fly out of the cage in a panic and scatter. It is so important for them to feel relaxed and confident when the door is finally opened and I have often sat for a couple of hours waiting for birds to leave their cage.

The morning was already quite warm and the day was promising to be quite a scorcher. I placed the cage down in a clearing, in the shade, then found myself a comfortable spot to sit and wait. After an hour or so the youngsters had settled enough for me to open their door. They would go back and forth to their food dishes, pausing frequently to look out the open door at their new surroundings. In all this time they had not made a sound. There wasn't a sign of any life, no birds were calling, only the endless whirr of the cicadas.

Another hour went by. I had been sitting, camera ready, watching keenly for something exciting to happen. By now it was getting quite hot and I was starting to get restless - almost to the point of boredom. The wrens would hop over to the open door, look out at that "big, scary world" and hop back onto a perch. Obviously preferring to look out from behind the safety of the wire.

I had focused the camera on a pile of fallen branches; a perfect resting place for little wrens. I was now quite uncomfortable - I was hot and my bottom ached from the hard ground.   To relieve the boredom I starting photographing some of the dead branches and sticks, imagining little birds resting on them. The surrounding bush was now completely still and even the cicadas were silenced by the heat.

Then Big flew out the door. He landed on a branch a few metres from the cage, confidently looked around and then flew back. He hopped about on the top of the cage, as though he was trying to encourage the other two to join him, then flew into a shrub calling softly to his siblings. Small flew out next and quickly joined Big. Poor Fluffy had been left behind and becoming agitated began calling frantically. Although they were still very close to the cage and Fluffy could see them, they refused to answer his calls. They were far too busy checking out their new environment. Fluffy was now getting extremely distressed and began calling louder and louder. Within seconds the bush came alive.

Red-backed wrens seemed to be everywhere, all calling. The racket these little birds made was amazing; the deathly silence only moments before be-came what appeared to be utter chaos. There was one adult male; very handsome in his black suit with its bright red collar, together with four brown birds. One of these had a bent tail, an indication that she had been sitting in a nest, the other three could have been females or juvenile males. They seemed unafraid of me and had come in quite close to 'check out the trou-ble'. During the excitement I had been madly photographing the action - and then I ran out of film. Worse, I had forgotten to put in spare rolls.

To make matters even more frustrating, two thornbills arrived to join in the ruckus and I looked up into the trees to see a female golden whistler. The

Male Red-backed Wren

Red-backed Wrens

bush was alive and I had no film! When a jenny wren perched sideways on a branch as though taunting me, I felt like screaming in frustration. She was so close I could have reached out and touched her. How I cursed myself for wasting so much film on those blasted sticks!

Although my wrens didn't seem nervous, I was beginning to feel a little apprehensive. I was unsure whether the wild birds were being aggressive; would they try and drive the intruders out of their territory or was the family here to help a distressed bird? Until now Fluffy had remained in the cage, still yelling his head off. Suddenly he flew out and landed near the wild birds. This was the big test. His brothers, seeing him out, flew across and joined the group. The young birds were darker in colour than the wild wrens and I had no trouble distinguishing them. The instant the three young birds were together the calls ceased. Immediately all the birds settled down, the thornbills lost interest and flew off. Then one of the wild females moved closer to the young strangers. It was a tense moment; would she attack or accept the intruders.

I'm still amazed when I recall that moment. The wild bird snuggled down into Fluffy and began preening him. It was almost as though she was reassuring him that everything was going to be alright. It was a sign of total acceptance into their family. Shortly after the adult male flew onto the same branch and after a quick check that all was now well, he twittered softly and flew back into the bush, leading the group away.

The release of the three red-backed wrens was the high point of my time spent with them. Never in my wildest dreams did I imagine they would be accepted so quickly into a wild family group, with me as a witness. By being accepted into the group their chance of survival was so much higher. If only I had not run out of film!

First Song

Lyn's Magpie

I may have devoted a complete book to the wonderful story of Lucky the wallaroo but the story of Maggie the white-backed magpie was just as unique as it was my first close encounter with a wild creature. How could I have guessed all those years ago that Maggie would influence me so much that I would throw away my career as a potter and become a wildlife painter whose favourite subject is magpies!

I first caught sight of Maggie on the side of a lonely road, standing stiffly to attention like a little black and grey soldier. Don, my husband, and I were driving through the bush on the New South Wales, Victorian border and had just come through a fierce electrical storm. The strong winds and bolts of lightning rocked the 4WD and the heavy rain made it difficult to see.

"Isn't that a baby magpie on the side of the road? Looks like he's in trouble!" said Don.

We peered through the window at the bedraggled little bird standing so straight and still at the base of a huge gum tree. There was no sign of any adult birds and the first branches of the tree looked to be at least ten metres above. The little fellow did not attempt to fly away when I came close to him nor did he struggle when I picked him up. Instead he looked at me with such trust that I was totally won over.

"He won't have a chance if we leave him here! Can we take him with us?" I wondered.

Of course we did take him with us and so began the wonderful relationship between this magpie and our family. He must have suffered on the long trip home to Nowra. Along the way we begged a box and some hamburger mince from a roadside shop and the little ball of feathers huddled away in the far corner of the box looking very miserable and scared. We were all too tired to worry about him when we finally got home so it was not until the next morning that we finally had a good look. Poor little magpie! Don and I and our daughter Merryon all peered into the box at once. This must have been terrifying but in spite of it he managed to return a bright and hopeful gaze.

"He doesn't look like the magpies round here with all that grey and white on his back. He must be a white-backed magpie." said Don.

Like all young magpies his downy grey chest feathers were textured with fine black and white marks and his wing feathers were a dark gun-metal grey. The fluffy feathers on his back were also finely textured but lighter because of the amount of white in the markings, a sign that he probably was a white-backed magpie and not a native of our area.

" Can we feed him before I go to school?" Merryon pleaded.

We had a nursery not far from the house so we started our search over there and after lifting a number of plant pots we came up with quite a good collection of insects and worms. We presented these proudly to the little magpie scattering them in the box.

He eyed them all wriggling around his feet and then looked up at us expectantly, as if to say, *Well your job isn't over yet!*

"He doesn't even know how to feed himself!" said a shocked Merryon.

We improvised with a plastic drinking straw, which was Merryon's idea, poking chopped up grubs into his open beak with it. This worked perfectly and we continued to use this method of feeding him until he became independent. I became chief feeder when everyone else got sick of hunting for insects and worms and his diet was expanded to include mincemeat, which was much easier to find!

As the little fledgling showed no signs of flying I took him and his box to my pottery shed to live. It seemed the best solution at the time with a cat that lived in the house and no birdcage. Looking back I think he became very lonely in the shed and even though I visited him regularly he seemed to lose his perky manner and became depressed as the days went by.

One day when Merryon and I and Sandy our dog went to visit the little magpie, we opened the door to find the shed empty.

"How on earth could he have escaped" I cried.

We searched every inch of the cluttered shed without finding even a feather and in desperation I said impatiently to Sandy, "Do something useful. Show how clever you are! Go find Maggie!"

Sandy was part dingo and clever as they come, so within seconds he was under one of my pottery tables sniffing around and looking up underneath the tabletop.

"Don't be silly Sandy! The little bird can't be under there!"

Of course I was wrong! The table had a drawer under it and when I pulled it out, there was Maggie huddled in a corner looking very frightened. I was never quite sure how he got into the drawer though it was just possible he had climbed in through a gap at the back. For a flightless bird this seemed hard to believe and I had a suspicion that he may have had some uninvited 'visitors' who had put him there or scared him so much he had climbed in there to hide. Whatever happened, he was not happy in the shed after this.

After worrying about Maggie for some time, I decided he must have more freedom and from then on I got up very early every morning and took him outside to the nursery. He would sit on my shoulder whilst we walked across to the shade house and then I would put him on the ground amongst the pots and we would spend the next hour hunting for his breakfast. As I lifted up a pot the little magpie would run over and eye off the treasures underneath looking just like an adult magpie searching for food. I am not an early riser but I loved this special time we shared in the mornings.

When we had exhausted ourselves and the supply of insects, he was put up on the overhead watering pipes which ran all over the nursery. Here he stayed most of the day, safe from dogs and cats on the ground and from birds overhead. He loved the nursery and the freedom he had there, but he never attempted to get down on the ground when I was not around. The fall from the nest may have made him cautious. In the late afternoon we would have another hunting session on the ground before he was put to bed on a pot plant 'tree' in our family room, well away from the cat.

While looking through my bird book to find out more about magpies I came to a surprise conclusion! Maggie was probably a girl. Lucky about her name! Maggie had lost her fluffy look and was developing into a sleeker bird whose chest feathers had become a subtle grey/black mottle. Her wing feathers had lengthened and the feathers on her back though whiter than her front, were

Singing Practise

strongly marked with black. A male white-backed magpie has a pure white back. From then on we wondered how we could have ever thought of her as a male when her mannerisms were so feminine and hen-like.

Whether Maggie was male or female, she certainly took her time learning to fly! In the end we decided we would have to teach her for her own safety. The resident black-backed magpies were an aggressive lot and not happy about the flightless little runt living in their territory, especially as the runt seemed to be over-indulged by the humans who shared their domain. Maggie did not help matters by calling out to them in a rude and taunting way from the safety of my shoulder, every time she saw them. It was only a matter of time before they taught her a lesson!

Our first attempts to get her airborn ended with undignified nosedives or belly landings. Even running along with Maggie perched on an outstretched arm did not give her the idea. We all tried. Merryon did the running and Don and I did the launching. Even throwing her gently into the air did not work. In desperation Don suggested we climb up on the brick barbecue and try launching her from there. At first we were hindered by two extra children who wanted to 'help'. Maggie refused to do anything while they watched and squawked abuse at them from my shoulder while I stood on top of the barbecue. It must have been a funny sight and I do not blame the children for wanting to be entertained but Maggie intended this to be a family affair only!

The first flight resulted in a pathetic flutter to the ground a few metres away but the second attempt was quite different. She must have felt the wind under her wings this time and after a bit of a wobble she took off. Amid screams and claps of approval from her family she flew over the roof of the house and out of sight. Finally she came back into view again flying in a graceful arc above our heads. She seemed to enjoy our shouts of encouragement and at that moment was the proudest magpie alive. For us it was like seeing a baby take her first steps and we were all relieved that our foster-bird could finally fly.

Maggie never looked back after that. She continued to sleep on her pot plant tree at night but spent her days outside hunting for insects, practising

her flying and getting into mischief. When we were out-side working she would always be close by amusing us with her comic behaviour. On the ground she did not look much like a wild bird and would run around like a fluffed up hen with her head down and tail up chasing insects, real or imaginary. If the dreaded black-backed magpie gang was around she would drop her wings, arch her neck and strut in a stiff-legged fashion fluffed up to twice her size. This was supposed to terrify the enemy magpies but they were probably laughing too.

If we sat on the grass with her she would immediately want to play, espe-cially with Merryon, who had a special relationship with her, being a child. First Maggie would prance around us and then roll on her back and wave her legs in the air as if she was peddling a bike upside down. She stayed in this position until one of us put out our hand, then she would grab hold of it with her upturned feet and allow herself to be lifted up, hanging upside down. She seemed quite happy to be carried around like this and once she was put down again would expect the game to be repeated! I have seen a pair of young magpies playing similar games in the wild. One would lie on its back and catch a low branch with its feet while the other sat on the branch, or they would both play/fight together in the same manner. The trouble with Maggie, she had to overdo everything and what was normal play developed into slap stick comedy.

"I hope the wild magpies aren't watching you now Maggie! They would fall off their branches laughing at you," we would warn her.

Once Maggie was free to come and go at will, our prime time with her was first thing in the morning when she came around to our bedroom and wolf whistled to be let in. She learnt this whistle from an early age and used it instead of the doorbell. She made for the bed once inside, and would find a hollow in the blanket between us, where she would settle down as though she was in a nest. We talked and she listened intently, every so often getting up and changing nesting places on the bed. During the day we had many visits from Maggie and she could always find us whatever room we were in. By walking up and down on the windowsill and wolf whistling she made sure she attracted our attention. Lunchtime was a favourite occasion for her. Don always had a rest on one of the lounges, and Maggie loved to sit on his chest and play with the hairs that stuck out over his collar, or if he had a really old shirt on, with the hairs that poked out through the holes! Sometimes she got really personal and moved up closer to his face.

"She's eyeing off your nose hairs Don! Look out or you'll have a beak up your nose!" I often had to warn. After this she usually settled down and had a quiet nap on Don's chest.

Visitors were a great attraction and it was very distracting to have a magpie eye-balling you through the window and making ear piercing wolf whistles while trying to make conversation. Usually we gave in and opened the window for her. She would make herself at home on the back of a couch and look intently from person to person as they spoke. Occasionally she left 'a calling card' down the back of a couch and if people arrived unexpectedly I needed to race in ahead of them and check out the couches for the odd 'decoration'.

The territorial magpies still kept Maggie on her toes. They lived in the tall gum trees that grew around the house and nursery and often she needed to duck for cover by flying into my work shed or the garage. If one of us was walking across the yard she often flew down and landed on our shoulder so that she could shout abuse at the enemy from the safety of her 'flock'. If I was wearing a long skirt, Maggie used it to hide under and would run along looking out from under the hem, all the time calling out rudely; *I have friends in high places and you nasty bunch of magpies had better watch out!*

Magpies have very strong beaks and can bite quite hard especially if they use the side of the beak to grip and twist. If Maggie disagreed with me about something she liked to lift a piece of skin on the back of my hand and twist! It hurt, but I tried not to let her know how much. She would look at my face intently while she was doing it as if to say, *You're supposed to yell like crazy when I do this. Others do!*

The 'others' were the two children Maggie had taken a dislike to. At first she just shrieked abuse at them but as time went by she bombarded them every time they came near the house. Eventually they both received the grab and twist treatment and became frightened of her. These chil-

Maggie

dren were the only victims Maggie ever chose to terrorize and I presume she had her reasons! Even so it was just as well we were planning to move to Queensland or their angry parents may have done something drastic.

We had no doubt that Maggie would come to Queensland with us. Things were getting too hot for her in Nowra anyway. Being semi-reliant on her family made her somewhat of a misfit but it did not occur to us that she could have gone back to her original habitat and been released there to take her chances. Today with more knowledge of the rescue and release of birds and animals I certainly would have taken her back and released her, but back then I knew very little about this kind of thing.

We set about planning our trip to south east Queensland where our house was being built in the Coomera Valley. Merryon and I were to take one car with Maggie and Bubby the cat and Don was to follow on later in the other car with Sandy. The journey was too long to tackle in one day so an over-night stop was planned, though just how we were going to manage that with a cat and a magpie was still a big question! On the first leg of the trip the cat meowed constantly and Maggie was ominously quiet. We poked pieces of meat through the holes in both boxes but were too cautious to open either of them. When we finally arrived at our half way point, Armidale, I sized up all the motels, looking for one that was impersonal enough in which to sneak a cat and a magpie. Unfortunately the room in the motel we chose was on the second floor and we had to creep up the back stairs with two suspicious looking cardboard boxes under our arms. We got to our room without bumping into anyone and without wasting any time, opened the boxes. The poor cat was still in a drugged state from the sedative I had given her and staggered out of her box looking very dishevelled. She swayed from side to side as she walked across the room with eyes half-closed and collapsed in a heap beside the bed. On the other hand Maggie was as lively as usual. She looked up at us with bright eyes and jumped up on the side of the box, dragging a towel with her. Unfortunately the towel I had put in the bottom of the box had some loose strands and these had become tangled around her feet. Though she had been very quiet all day she must have moved around a lot to do this and her feet looked swollen and sore. Merryon and I anxiously unravelled the threads and at last she was free and able to fly onto my shoulder. Of course she was very hungry and thirsty but also very interested in her new

surroundings. While I was wondering where to put her for the night she solved my problem by flying into the bathroom and perching on the shower rail. I turned the light out quickly so she would stay there and go to sleep. When we were cleaning our teeth later, in the dark, she kept peering down at us as if to say, "Why don't you turn the light on?" Needless to say we did not have a shower that night!

Merryon and I giggled together nervously as we went to bed. Having a magpie in the bathroom and a cat under the bed was not normal behaviour for us when we stayed in motels.

"I hope Maggie doesn't start singing as soon as it gets light. Someone will tell the manager and then he'll find we've got a cat as well" Merryon worried.

"We'll take off at the first sound of a warble. I'm sure we can make a fast get away!" I reassured her feeling a bit like a criminal!

We slipped away at first light with neither of our charges giving us away and reached our destination without incident.

The house was well behind schedule and still had about four weeks to go before the building was completed. Fortunately the garage was finished and our plan was to keep the two pets and Maggie in there until they got used to the place. It sounded like a crazy plan, shutting a cat and dog up with a bird but it worked! The pets knew Maggie was part of their family and I did not have to leave them shut up for long. Maggie was used to her new home in a couple of days and was free to come and go from then on. Sandy of course became king of his castle right away, marking out his territory very thoroughly but poor Bubby hid in the garage and was traumatized for weeks.

When we finally moved in, Maggie seemed happier and freer than she had been in our old home. The land had formerly been an old dairy farm where all the original rainforest had been cleared. A pair of butcher birds and a noisy family of kookaburras shared this with us, but there were no territorial magpies. Today we have re-established a lot of the rainforest and as a consequence have a great many more birds, but in those days it was just nine acres of grass and a couple of trees, stretching down to a river.

Maggie had loved living on a building site. The more trucks, workmen,

Howdy Rowdy - Kookaburras

equipment and commotion the better. She greeted each workman with her best wolf whistle, checking out the backs of their trucks, following them around, having a good time and getting in the way. In return the workmen enjoyed having a bit of entertainment while they worked, shared their lunch with her and stopped work to watch every time she did something funny. The carpenters were her best friends as they were there the longest and she plagued them constantly. She would pick up the screw or nail they were just about to use and fly off with it or perch on the top of their ladder and knock off all the things they had put within reach. I am sure the carpentry took twice as long because of Maggie! On one occasion, in a heavy downpour of rain, Maggie found a tub of water and proceeded to have a bath. As usual she was 'over the top' with her antics, fluffing up to twice her size, spraying water out in all directions and jumping in and out of the tub in a most theatrical way. She had attracted a large audience of workmen and was enjoying every minute like a true entertainer.

When the building was finished Maggie spent her days happily flying free, coming back for food and company and of course getting into mischief. We had built a covered garden surrounded by the house on three sides and it was here that she safely roosted at night. She still paid her early morning calls to our bedroom for a chat and a nest on the bed and she still demanded to be let in if the company looked interesting, but she spent more time on her own outside.

Getting into mischief was still high on Maggie's agenda and she was often too inquisitive for her own good. Pieces of string and rope were favourite playthings. She would watch closely when we were staking up young trees and as soon as there was a loose piece of string lying around she would snatch it up and trot off dragging the string behind. One day I found her hopelessly tangled in a fishing line which had been left outside. She had

probably tried to pull out a strand to play with and ended up with the line wrapped around her feet. How defenceless she looked standing there unable to move. I was surprised that she had not panicked. She looked up at me trustingly as if to say, *You can fix it.*

"What if I hadn't found you Maggie! You could

have died of hunger or something could have killed you!" I worried. After I untangled her she trotted off happily looking for something else to 'sticky beak' into.

The cat's tail was an entertaining plaything for Maggie too. Bubby enjoyed lying outside in the driveway and as soon as she got settled and had fallen asleep Maggie would come up behind and study the tail. Apparently it was not interesting unless it was moving so she would wait until the cat felt herself being watched and began to twitch her tail. Maggie would then chase the tail back and forth as it twitched, pecking the end of it with her beak. This annoyed Bubby and she would get up and move to another part of the drive-way where she would flop down and go to sleep again and Maggie's tail game could start all over again.

I worried that Maggie's curiosity would be the end of her. When she disap-peared for two days I imagined terrible situations that could have befallen her. Was she shut in someone's shed after going in to investigate or was she dying of exposure tangled up in something? I was just about to go and ask all my neighbours if they had seen her when she arrived back on my kitchen windowsill looking a bit the worse for wear. No wolf whistles this time, only a dash to the water bucket where she perched and drank a very long draught. "I don't know what happened Maggie, but being nosey will surely be the end of you" I warned.

Her inquisitive nature was helpful on some occasions. One day she flew up to me in a great state of panic while I was working in the garden. She squawked and flapped her wings at me in an agitated way and then flew off a short distance as if she wanted me to follow. When I caught up with her she re-peated the behaviour, leading me further and further down the paddock. Finally she landed on the grass near something that was hanging from the barbed wire fence. As I got closer the thing began to flutter and I could see it was another magpie with its legs tangled in something that had caught on the fence. Maggie stood there looking at the entangled magpie and calling to it when I caught up. I could imagine her saying, *See, I said I'd come back with someone to help you. I've got some pretty useful friends you know!*

How long the magpie had been there I could not tell but the strands of shade cloth had cut into its feet and made them quite swollen. I threw my shirt over the magpie and cut the strands away from the fence but I needed to take it up to the house to untangle the mess of threads around its feet. It took a long time to pull all the strands away with tweezers and scissors. Maggie supervised the whole thing from my shoulder and looked as pleased as I did when we finished bathing the magpie's feet and took it back to the paddock to let it go. It was moments like these that made me realize how much I loved Maggie as I walked back with her on my shoulder, knowing we had shared a good deed together.

It was during this time that we were visited by a large flock of young magpies; probably about ten to fifteen young birds. It was the only time in all the years we have been here that it happened and a lucky break for Maggie. They loved the open paddocks but were friendly enough to come right up to the house for a feed. They may have felt more confident because they saw Maggie close to the house and also riding around on our shoulders. Whatever the reason, we were pleased to have them about, for her sake. Maggie loved this flock of teenagers and spent all her time with them, happy at last to be part of a flock. Her best friend was a bird we called 'Beaky,' for obvious reasons. His feathers were still textured with grey and white but he was sleek and handsome and we hoped he might become Maggie's mate. Her adult plumage and odd hen-like mannerisms meant she stood out from the group but they seemed to accept her. We hoped they would stay, as Maggie was the happiest she had ever been.

Unfortunately, as quickly as the flock arrived, it was gone, and Maggie was on her own again. I'm sure she missed them and probably would have gone too if the tie with us had not been so strong. To make matters worse a mating pair of magpies staked a claim to the territory near our house not long after and Maggie had to be on guard once again. She worked out a strategy and most of the time she avoided the pair, but the halcyon days were over.

One day when Don was bagging up seed he noticed Maggie picking up short pieces of rope and flying up to a nearby tree with them.
"I think Maggie's trying to build a nest" Don laughed.
"Why would she want to build a nest? She hasn't even got a mate!" I answered.

Magpie Teenagers

The next time she picked up a piece of rope I followed her. Sure enough, in a most unsuitable gum tree, she had built a large nest of sticks and was lining it with the pieces of rope she was stealing from Don. The gum tree was just a large sapling and the nest was only about three metres above the ground but she had chosen a good fork in the tree and the nest looked sturdy and strong. We teased some rope out into finer strands and left it in a pile for her and within a few hours it was all gone and Maggie was established on her nest! "Surely she's not going to lay eggs. How can she do that without a mate?" I wondered.

Maggie sat on the nest for days, occasionally getting up and turning round in circles before fluffing up her feathers and sitting down again. She looked over the edge of the nest with a very proud look in her eye when I came over to talk to her and give her a feed. I did not take her seriously until the day I climbed the ladder to have a look while she was away somewhere and found she had laid two eggs! I could not believe my eyes and decided they must be infertile with no sign of a mate around.

"How will she be able to protect the eggs without a mate? The crows will get them if a goanna doesn't beat them to it! I'll have to help her." I said.

Maggie's tree became a sight to behold once I got into action. I wrapped barbed wire around the trunk of the tree like a collar to stop anything climbing up and pitched a brightly coloured umbrella above the nest so crows could not see it. It was a funny sight and drew an audience for a few days but of course Maggie did not mind and kept sitting on her eggs looking like a contented hen. It is sight I will always cherish as it was the last time I saw Maggie.

Some days later we noticed Maggie was not on her nest and when I climbed up the ladder to look for her eggs they were gone too. The nest stayed in the tree for a long time after I took the umbrella and the barbed wire down and was a constant reminder that Maggie was no longer with us. She had been our constant companion for three years and the gap she left in our lives was considerable. For months after I would think I heard her wolf whistle and race outside expecting to see her strutting up and down on the window sill in her comical way. Even today when I least expect it, the warble of a magpie can make my heart turn over.

Sometime later I went to the art exhibition of a well-known wildlife artist and was confronted by a painting of a white-backed magpie. To make it even more poignant there was a comment beside the painting describing how the artist had seen the subject northwest of Brisbane and how he wondered why a white-backed magpie could be so far from home. I was convinced it was Maggie and when I finally caught up with the artist we had a long talk about the possibility of her travelling to that area and if white-backed magpies ever mated with black-backed ones. We did not resolve anything of course, but it gave me hope. Maybe Maggie is still out there somewhere trotting around like a hen and proudly laying fertile eggs now.

I have painted a lot of magpie pictures over the years even though people said that magpie subjects would not sell. I am pleased to prove them wrong and pleased to find that there are so many magpies lovers around with wonderful stories like mine to tell.

Feed Me! - White-breasted Woodswallows

UFO

My first introduction to UFO came when Margaret, a close friend and wildlife carer asked me to identify a baby bird she had in her care - "an unidentified flying object." I immediately recognized him as a white-breasted woodswallow as I had previously seen these babies. He had been picked up on the ground at a busy service station right beside a highway. It is possible that he was the last baby to fledge and was not strong enough to keep up with the rest of the family, so the decision was made to keep him in care. Although a common species that is widely distributed over much of Australia, woodswallows do not come into care very often.

So here we had a single woodswallow with the very slim chance of finding another fledgling of his kind and all the possibilities of him bonding too closely with his carer. Not a good prospect for eventual release! But the little fellow was in good health, eating well, with bright eyes looking round in the inquisitive manner of his kind and seeming none the worse for his ordeal. Inspite of his solitary existence he became a delightful character inventing games and toys for himself and even a pretend sibling to cuddle up to. He became the subject of quite a few of my paintings and amazed me with his ability to adjust and make the most of life on his own.

Due to their habit of catching the majority of their food (mainly insects) in

flight, woodswallows need a great deal of exercise. Because of UFO's trusting nature and the threat of attack from butcher birds, Margaret was reluctant at the time to put him outside in an aviary. She solved the problem by allowing him out of his cage each morning and afternoon to fly freely in the safety of the house. Margaret's home remained cobweb free with UFO around. He would pick any spiders out of their webs and then perch on Margaret's shoulder to eat his meal. Margaret didn't mind UFO's house cleaning skills but she really wasn't too happy about being used as his dinner table.

Like many of our birds, UFO liked to play with "toys". These were kept in a basket near his cage and when he was let out for his flying exercises he would go to his basket to pick out a toy with which to play. One of his toys was a small twisted piece of paper (like a butterfly) which he would take in his beak, sit on the top of his cage and proceed to "kill", chattering away nonstop and warning anyone not to come too near! By far, his favourite toys were his collection of ribbons. With a ribbon held firmly in his beak, he would fly around the room, then drop the ribbon and chase it as it fell, catching it before it landed on the floor. This game would be repeated many times with UFO obviously enjoying himself immensely.

UFO also liked to 'help' Noel, Margaret's husband, with his crossword puzzles. He would chase after the pen while Noel wrote, every so often stopping to try and remove the 'words' from the page. He also enjoyed 'jigsaw puzzle time', but became a nuisance when he began thieving pieces and flying off, depositing them in hidden corners of the house. Eventually, after UFO had lost a few pieces, Margaret had to cover any exposed puzzles; hiding them from prying eyes.

It was his stealing habit that was almost UFO's undoing and ended with him being rushed to the vet! Margaret's mother, Evelyn who was visiting, had been put in charge of supervising UFO's playtime while her daughter was busy feeding her other birds. Evelyn loved to knit and she noticed UFO had stolen a strand of wool and had started to swallow it. Even though she quickly tried to catch UFO and retrieve the wool he was not about to give up his new toy and kept out of reach until he had swallowed all six inches of it! After a frantic phone call to the vet, UFO was rushed in with the hope that the wool could be removed before it caused a blockage. However the vet could see no sign of anything, the wool had vanished. UFO sat quietly in his cage for the next twenty four hours, Margaret was sure he was starting to look ill and Evelyn was blaming herself for not watching him more closely. I think UFO was looking smug!

Many insectivorous birds regurgitate undigested food (insect shells etc) in pellet form, which is called a 'casting'. The following morning Margaret

noticed one on the floor of UFO's cage and as she picked it up to remove it, she caught a glimpse of something red. Closer inspection revealed the strand of stolen wool; regurgitated intact. UFO had obviously decided he had finished with his toy and had finally given it up.

Because wooodswallows are a flock bird and when resting, snuggle tightly together, I suggested to Margaret that the young bird might need something to cuddle into to help him settle at night. UFO got a little red teddy! He became very attached to his cosy little "friend" and when Margaret took Teddy away to give him a much needed bath UFO would become quite upset. Until Teddy was returned, UFO would sit huddled up on his perch in a sulk. One particular time when Teddy took longer than usual to dry UFO became so upset that Margaret had to squeeze as much water out as she could and return Teddy to the cage , clean but still damp. It is possibly the sweetest thing I have ever seen, that little grey and white bird snuggled tightly into the arms of his little red teddy.

UFO had imprinted very badly on humans and although he was capable of catching his own food Margaret became quite concerned about his eventual release. This was brought home with a jolt when Margaret and her husband Noel had to go away for a couple of weeks. I had offered to mind UFO as I was familiar to him and we did not think he would become too distressed.

UFO went on a hunger strike! The only way I could get him to eat was to

hand feed him; little bits at a time, up to a dozen times a day for the first few days. He did eventually start to settle, but still only ate half-heartedly by himself, with me 'topping him up'. As soon as he heard Margaret's voice, when she arrived to pick him up, he went frantic, calling to her non-stop. We let him out of the cage and he flew straight onto Margaret's shoulder, snuggling into her neck and chattering away the whole time. I am sure he was telling her that I had tried to starve him!

* * *

UFO had been in care a full year when Margaret was lucky enough to get another woodswallow fledgling. At first UFO ignored the little stranger but curiosity started to get the better of him and he began to answer the baby's calls. Eventually Margaret decided to let the two birds out of their cages together. UFO continued to ignore the other bird but did not act aggressively towards it. Being only a baby, the newcomer began to make the first advances. For Margaret it was a tense time, if UFO accepted the other bird it meant he had a good chance of full rehabilitation and could be released back into the wild. As luck would have it Margaret received another two woodswallow fledglings. As often happens when more than one bird of the same species are raised together these birds do not imprint on humans, but bond instead with each other. Consequently, when fully fledged they can become quite wild and are a better prospect for release.

Eventually, UFO's affections were directed mainly towards the other young birds. Although he remained confiding with Margaret, he became either aloof or nervous when strangers were around. UFO had crossed the line and bonded with his own species and now had a chance of a normal life. The little red teddy was no longer needed!

I'm Watching You-Tawny Frogmouths

Tawny Tales

I have often been asked what is my favourite bird to have in care and without hesitation I can answer, "The tawny frogmouth." Although we have had so many wonderful individuals, full of personality, from different species, the tawny frogmouths as a group are for me the most endearing.

The majority of the adults are placid amiable birds that are extremely easy to work with, through the day sitting quietly in their cages. They rely heavily on their mottled plumage for camouflage and rather than flapping around in their cages in an attempt to get away, will adopt a pose resembling a dead branch. And the fledglings would have to be the most captivating baby birds you would ever wish to see. They look as though their closest relative should be a muppet, not a bird. When they are sitting on a branch with their eyes closed you could easily mistake them for a pale grey pom pom made of feathers. When they open their brilliant yellow eyes the effect can be quite startling, "Oh my goodness, it's alive!" you want to exclaim.

Although often called 'frogmouth owls' they are not owls at all, but a large member of the nightjar family. Like owls, the nightjars are nocturnal (birds of the night), however unlike owls the frogmouths are not a bird of prey. Their feet are small and quite puny; totally unsuitable for grasping and killing prey. Instead they rely on their huge beak and gape - 'hence frogmouth' - to catch and feed predominantly on insects, frogs and occasionally small mammals.

It is their habit of feeding on insects on the edges of roads at night which brings so many of these birds to grief. Through the summer months adult frogmouths can be one of the most common species in care - victims of car accidents. If the birds are lucky they are only stunned and can usually be returned, a day or two later, to where they were found. Unfortunately, too many suffer from broken wings or backs, or the injury I am most fearful of - a damaged lens in the eye. This can be difficult to treat and if too much damage has occurred the bird can be permanently blinded.

I will always remember the night when our local rural fire brigade paid me a visit. The firemen were returning from a call when an adult frogmouth flew into the windscreen of the firetruck. Three of the men, with soot covered faces, were standing in my kitchen watching as I went over the bird, assessing his injuries. Their concern was genuine and I was quite touched when they apologised for hitting him. Unfortunately, the tawny had suffered extensive injuries and those three burly men looked totally crushed when I told them that I didn't think there was much I could do to save his life. Sadly the bird died not long after they left, but the care shown by those busy men was truly heart-warming.

As I said earlier, the majority of wild, adult tawnys can be placid amiable birds. Rarely do they try and use their massive beak as a weapon and they *never* roll over on their backs and strike viciously with their feet. Those who have had a harmless looking noisy miner grasp their hand in its feet and dig needle sharp claws into their flesh will know just how excruciatingly painful it can be! The tawny's main defence is to open his beak, showing the enormous yellow gape and occasionally he will emit a scream; a harsh, rasping cry that can be a bit nerve wracking to the uninitiated.

Now, having said all that...... the worst injury I have ever sustained from any animal I have had in my care, was from a tawny frogmouth we called Uncle Fester. Fester had been caught in a barbed wire fence, suffering a very badly injured wing. However, even though we had treated the wing, the infection appeared to be getting worse and it was necessary to take him back to the vet. I was lifting Fester out of his cage when he turned his head and suddenly chomped down on my thumb. His wing must have been extremely sore and he held on tightly to my thumb, sawing the sharp edge of his beak back and forth, not releasing his grip until I had put him in his carry box. I gave my hand a good shake and then inspected my thumb to see what damage he had done. The skin had barely been broken - it was not even bleeding - so, deciding there was nothing worth worrying over, I promptly forgot about it.

The following day my thumb was still feeling a bit sore but once again I dismissed it thinking it was a bit of bruising. However, later the following night it really started to throb - similar to the throb when you've slammed your thumb in a door. By morning my hand was aching and I noticed a red line of infection from my thumb down into my palm. Off to the doctor I went and ended up on antibiotics for six weeks before the infection cleared up. In that period my thumb had swollen to twice its normal size; the skin had become red and blistered and I couldn't hold anything in my hand. During one of my check-ups, my doctor, who was quite fascinated by this reaction to the bite, called in one of his colleagues to have a look too. After much oohing and aahing she looked up at me and said "I have seen infection similar to this once before, but that bite was from a goanna!"

Obviously bacteria from Fester's infected wing had entered through that tiny break in the skin. It was a lesson well learned though. Any bites are now washed - scrubbed if necessary - immediately. Unfortunately, poor Uncle Fester died the same day he had bitten me. As you can imagine I became the butt of quite a few jokes, "Did you hear about the bird that bit Peta? It died!"

Of all the frogmouths I have had in care, Hi-me (from Get Smart), was our most memorable character. His nest had been blown out of a tree during a storm and he was the smallest baby frogmouth I had raised at the time. About a week after he arrived he had grown enough to leave his artificial nest and sit on a broad branch. He was a delight to have in the studio while I worked,

sitting quietly on his perch looking like an ornament. When he started to get hungry his body would start to sway as he shifted back and forth on his feet, his head would begin to bob and he would make a low "ooom". Never demanding like other baby birds. Just a patient "Could you please feed me?"After his morning and afternoon feeds he would lie down across his branch and have a nap. This is a common habit with young tawnys and the reason why I always provide them with a broad, heavy branch, low to the floor of the cage, to perch on.

Hi-me grew rapidly into one of the largest and most

Owlet Nightjar

handsome frogmouths I have raised, or had in care. He was a magnificent bird. His plumage was very dark brown and with his large head, massive beak and enormous yellow eyes, he was most impressive. Often during the day he would sprawl himself across the sand floor in the aviary, sunbaking. He loved a shower from the hose on a hot day; spreading his wings, fanning his tail and tilting his head back, he would move slowly around under the water. It was like a strange exotic dance and very beautiful to watch. Prior to his release I began to take his food into the aviary at night. It is an eerie feeling to be standing there in the dark and having a large bird suddenly and silently appear beside you, uttering a deep oom, oom, oom.

One evening when I was down in the aviary with Hi-me, I was treated to a rare sight. I'd heard a soft twittering and turned in time to catch a glimpse of a small bird with a long tail, land in a tree just outside the aviary. Thinking it was strange for a willie-wagtail to be flying around at night I turned the torch onto the branch where the bird had landed. It wasn't a willie at all. It was an owlet nightjar, our smallest member of the nightjar family. Although common, these small birds are rarely seen as they roost in a hollow during the day, only coming out after dark. The little bird was quite unafraid and I was able to have a really good look at him; the large dark eyes and whiskery face making him look more like a mammal than a bird. As I stood there admiring him I was reminded of Ollie. This little nightjar had got himself stuck during the night to the wet paint on a newly painted tractor. He suffered the loss and damage to quite a few feathers and remained in care until these regrew. He was an excellent patient and eventually he made a full recovery and was returned to the wild - hopefully avoiding wet paint in the future.

Hi-me had been a 'late summer' baby and I had held him over through the winter months. The following spring I was confident that Hi-me was ready to be released. As we live in an area with a lot of bush around us I was able to release Hi-me at home. This is always preferable as I can then keep an eye on the birds, if they stay, and supplement feed them if they need it. I carried Hi-Me out of the aviary and put him onto a branch in a big, old grevillea that was growing nearby. He began waddling along the branch and seemed quite

Night Watchman- Tawny Frogmouth

unperturbed by his new surroundings. Suddenly he dropped his head to the branch, opened his beak and began moving it back and forth along the limb. I had read that frogmouths will glean insects in this manner from branches, but I had never witnessed it before and felt quite thrilled to get a chance to watch this behaviour. It was also encouraging to know that Hi-me still had the instinct to forage as this would supplement his diet while he learnt to hunt.

Eventually, Hi-me flew off into the darkness and I wondered (and worried) if he would be O.K. and if he would be back. Hi-me did return. The following night, Josh was lying on the floor, reading in front of the open sliding door. Suddenly there was a whoosh of wings against the screen. Josh leapt to his feet and face pale, looked out into the dark, "What was that?" he asked nervously. Trying to hold back my laughter I walked across to the door and turned on the outside light. There was Hi-me sitting proudly and confidently on the back of one of the outside chairs - and I'm sure he was smiling.

Hi-me took a couple of pieces of meat from me, then spotting a movement on the lawn he flew down and caught something. I was unable to see what it was but at least I had seen him hunting. He also didn't appear to be very hungry so I felt sure he was catching his own food. He returned each night for a couple of weeks; always to the same chair on the verandah. Sometimes he would take food, but mostly he seemed to be using the chair as a vantage point to spot what was happening on the ground. I felt very pleased with his hunting techniques when my neighbours told me they had been awakened one night by a thumping on their roof. When they went outside to see what it was they were greeted by the sight of Hi-me holding a large, green frog in his beak; banging it vigorously on the roof. I am fortunate to have tolerant neighbours, who like birds. It wasn't long after this that Hi-me stopped his nocturnal visits.

The following year a pair of frogmouths nested in a tree in our garden. They successfully raised two young that year and the year after, before moving away. During this time the large male would often perch not far from the ground and we could approach quite close before he became 'a stick'. These birds rely very heavily on their camouflage and this behaviour could have been normal for a wild bird. However, we like to think it was Hi-me and he had come home.

Snappy Dresser- Spangled Drongo

The Drongo

I had just finished preparing the evening meal and as I walked to the door to call Denis inside, I paused in wonder at the scene before me. Denis had his back to me and was leaning on the timber fence rail that surrounds our paddock. Our old horse stood on the other side of the fence, our kelpie, Dusty, sat at his feet and a medium sized, glossy black bird was perched on the rail at his elbow. The bird was closely watching and mimicking any movements Denis made. When Denis looked at the ground, the bird also looked at the ground. When Denis nodded his head, the bird would nod his head as though agreeing with whatever it was that was being said. Occasionally I could hear the soft murmur of their voices, the bird's strange metallic "Uh huh?", as though he was asking a question. The setting sun had illuminated the feathers on the bird's back giving them a beautiful iridescent blue sheen. The two of them, man and bird, looked for all the world just like a pair of old mates spending a quiet moment together, reflecting on the events of their day. It's a memory I will always hold very dear.

The bird was a young spangled drongo I had raised and a more confiding, entertaining bird I have yet to meet. After his release he adapted easily to life in the wild and although he was always 'his own bird' he remained friendly and sociable towards humans. There were many times I had the feeling we were only another toy for him to tease and harass, but mostly, I think he just liked people.

When I received the drongo into care he was quite a large baby, just fledged, and it wasn't long before he began to feed himself. As I had so little contact with him I was sure he wouldn't become imprinted and should eventually become quite wild. We didn't even give him a name, usually referring to him as The Drongo, and after his release a few other choice names as well. This was one bird with a definite mind of his own. He didn't become imprinted, but he didn't become 'wild' either.

Whilst in the aviary he remained a little on the aloof side. On the rare occasion he had sat on my back when I was cleaning out his cage. For most of the day he liked to perch on the ledge above the door and would often watch in interest as I hung out the washing. However, if I walked across to him and put my hand on the wire he would make aggressive attempts to bite me, often grabbing the wire in his beak and growling! The feathers on each side of his head had grown quite long and he could raise and lower these at will. When raised they gave the appearance of great bushy eyebrows - his Robert Menzies look. And when he was being naughty, and those feathers were raised, he looked just like a little devil!

The first two attempts at releasing the drongo were disastrous. On both occasions he was attacked and driven to the ground by a flock of our resident noisy miners. Both times I had to step in and rescue him, putting him back in the aviary where it was safe. However, although I felt discouraged, I did persevere and on the third attempt he was released just before daybreak - before the other birds were awake. There was only one miner out and about that morning (the early bird catches the worm) and when he swooped down at the drongo, the drongo was able to hold his own with ease. He stayed around in the garden for a couple of hours, occasionally getting into a bit of a scrap with the miners and once with one of the resident butcher birds. However, each time he was threatened he stood his ground and eventually the other birds left him alone and went about their own business. I was feeling quite confident that the release was successful when he disappeared. "Oh well, I guess that's another bird I'll wonder about" I said to myself.

Early the following morning, while I was feeding the birds, the drongo arrived back. I was thrilled to see that he was looking well and only slightly nervous, keeping a good eye on those annoying noisy miners. Thinking he might be hungry, I offered him food and he snatched it greedily from my hand. He then followed along behind me as I went to the different cages, giving everyone their breakfast. While I fed the horse he sat on the fence, watching intently. "Come on then," I called to him as I headed back to the house, "I'll put some breakfast out for you too."

The pattern was set. Each morning my little black friend would be waiting for me to come outside. He would then fly along beside me as I fed the other animals. The cats detested him. We lock them in their own 'aviary' at night and let them out again in the morning. The drongo would sit and wait for them to appear and then ' bomb' them as soon as they stepped outside. Nerves shattered, fur standing on end, the cats would quickly race for shelter inside the house. As soon as the cats were safely out of the way he would turn his attention to driving off the dog, who liked to join me on my morning rounds. Dusty's tactic was to ignore him and it was so amusing to watch her trot along, nose in the air, with that pesky bird bouncing backwards and forwards off the top of her head.

After the morning feeds were done it was time for him to help peg out the washing. Each peg, when put on the line, was inspected thoroughly and any loose ends of clothing were grabbed in his beak to have a quick game of tug-of-war. The morning he had a quick bath in the pool and perched on the clothes line, spreading his wings and fanning his tail - hanging himself out to dry - I could barely contain my laughter.

For the drongo, life was all about having fun, one big game. Whenever we were out in the garden the drongo would join us. If we swam in the pool, so did the drongo. He loved nothing better than a game of pool basketball and would chase endlessly after the ball as it was thrown back and forth. If I was weeding the garden he would sit beside me (or on my lap) waiting in antici-pation for any tasty morsel I might find him. It was not unusual to be doing the watering with the drongo sitting on my head. He would constantly chat-ter away to us in his strange metallic voice, finishing each sentence with a querulous "Uh huh?"

Our garden quickly became the drongo's domain and he lorded it over any of the other avian visitors. The noisy miners had soon been put in their place and I did feel sorry for the rosellas and king parrots when they visited the feeder. It the drongo was in good humour he would leave them alone, how-ever, most of the time he would swiftly send them on their way. He had an uneasy truce with the magpies and butcher birds and would only rarely make a half-hearted attempt at 'picking a fight' before he quickly ducked for cover.

It was a wonderful moment for me the day Norman, a currawong I had

raised and released, paid a visit. Norman had been living as a wild bird for three years and although he still called in on the odd occasion, he had become very timid. This was the first time he had been back since the drongo's release and the smaller black bird quickly spotted the new intruder and moved in for a closer look. As soon as I produced the mealworm container Norman flew straight down to me, and although nervous, began taking the food from my hand.

Within seconds the drongo had joined us - anything for a free meal. He stood on the ground beside Norman, keeping one wary eye on the larger bird and the other on the mealworms. The pair of them looked like David and Goliath, but their manners were impeccable; waiting patiently side by side as I passed a mealworm one at time to each bird in turn. The moment was particularly poignant for me as Styles had only recently died and his death had affected me far more deeply than I could ever have imagined. I relished the trust and friendship shown by these two free living birds; birds I had raised and set free now feeding so quietly beside each other. It was a real lift to my spirits and just when I thought things couldn't be better, Norman took my hand in his beak to initiate the 'tug-of-war-with-my-beak' game. But, 'magic moments' don't last forever and eventually Norman had had enough and flew back up into the trees, hotly pursued by the drongo. Poor Norman was then subjected to a barrage of aerial assaults until he finally moved on.

Unlike a lot of birds, the drongo liked children. As far as he was concerned they were just another human to entertain him and a favourite game was 'chasey'. When Ryan arrived home from school in the afternoon he would race outside calling "Come on Snoop" (Ryan's pet name for him). He would then race off around the garden, the drongo flying after him. Eventually, exhausted, Ryan would collapse on the ground laughing and panting. The drongo would be perched nearby, also panting, and I'm sure if he was able he would have been laughing too. There was no malice in the game, it was just pure good fun.

Although quite capable of catching his own food, the drongo still relied on (and expected) a handout. Each morning, when I was feeding the other birds, he would arrive for his breakfast. Each morning that is except for Sunday. Sunday mornings were a mystery to us and we never did find out where he would disappear to. We often joked that he had gone to church. I

did become concerned though when he hadn't reappeared one Sunday afternoon and on the Monday morning when he still hadn't arrived I really started to worry. He had been flying freely at that stage for over three months and it was getting close to the time of the year when many drongos migrate. I tried to convince myself that maybe this was the case. However, he arrived back on the Tuesday morning and my initial fears had been well founded; one wing had been injured and although it wasn't broken his flying ability had been impaired. At the time I thought he may have interfered in a fight between our resident magpies and the transient currawongs - an ongoing battle fought each year just before winter.

For most of the day, the drongo sat around quietly and I put extra food out for him as I didn't think he would be able to catch enough on his own. He really was feeling very sorry for himself and it was sad to see a little of his old spark go out. However, the next day his wing had become worse and I noticed he had difficulty flying in a straight line and he had a lot of trouble getting any height. I reluctantly decided to recapture him and put him back in the aviary. This would then allow him to rest the wing properly and was also for his own safety.

It was no trouble to catch him (while he sat on my hand I walked into the aviary), but I hated seeing him locked up again. Unfortunately, it took nearly a month for the wing to heal and by then it was too late in the season to let him go. I decided to keep him there until Spring when the migrating drongos returned for the Summer. I tried to make the aviary as interesting as possible for him; supplying him with fresh branches every few days, and gave him a bell on a chain to play with. When his wing had healed I would throw small sticks or food in the air for him to chase and catch, a game he always enjoyed. However, it wasn't quite the same as flying freely and often he would sit on a branch near the front of the aviary looking out at the sky. He must have been nearly bored out of his mind. I recalled how, when he was free, he would become bored and naughty on rainy days, constantly tormenting our caged birds. He had learnt early that the rainbow lorikeets would bite his feet if he perched on the wire of their cages. However, if he sat on the towels that cover the top they couldn't get him and he would pull the towel back just enough so that he could then poke his beak through the wire and tease them in safety. Poor Eric (the Indian Ringneck) was a different matter. Eric has a large cocky cage and the drongo would leap around on the top, pulling at Eric's toys through the bars. Unfortunately, for Eric, he is not as quick with his beak as the lorikeets and on wet days the drongo would torment him for hours.

Eventually, the dullness of his days back in captivity began to take its toll and the drongo started to become irritable and snappy with us. Whenever I started to leave the aviary he would fly at my hand, grabbing it as though begging me to stay. With Denis he was worse and after he had drawn blood a couple of times, Denis refused to go in the aviary with him. He would even scream abuse at him when Denis walked past the aviary and I remembered the dreadful tantrum the drongo threw the day I spotted him on a bench in the garage.

He had found an open container of screws and washers and was having a wonderful time throwing them all over the place. He watched intently as I started picking them up (calling him a few choice names) and each time I tried to put them in the box he would throw them back out again. Then I noticed a small screw clutched tightly in his foot. Thinking it wasn't a safe toy for him to have, I quickly snatched it away from him. In a flash his mood changed. Screaming abuse, he poked his beak at my hand, trying desperately to retrieve his treasure. Even as I was putting the container away out of reach he continued his yelling and his attacks on my hand. I had previously seen similar behaviour when he had been chasing an insect and had been unable to catch it. The same abusive language was used as he flew after the bug and when his efforts proved futile he flew across to a shrub and proceeded to vent his anger on it, tearing at the leaves and throwing them to the ground!

It was during this period of incarceration that I began getting reports about just how far this friendly black bird had been travelling when he had been free. I knew he had been calling in on our immediate neighbours, but I was surprised to learn he had been visiting houses up to a kilometre away. There was one home he visited regularly and would sit in their office, happily sorting through the paperwork. We had tried to discourage him from coming inside our home but there had been the odd occasion when he had flown through an open door. We still chuckle about the day he grabbed an envelope in the studio and flew off with it - air mail. When I heard he had been going for early morning 'walks' with people out walking their dogs, I recalled the afternoon when he had joined me. I had walked to the end of our street to photograph a red-flowering eucalyptus. Unexpectedly he had landed on my shoulder, giving me quite a start, before flying onto a branch of the tree I was photographing. As he sat amongst the beautiful red blossom I remember feeling so proud of the handsome bird he had become.

The more I heard about his adventures the more I began to worry, and seeds of doubt about how safe this area was for the drongo began to form in my mind. I was no longer comfortable with releasing him again here at home. I wondered too if his injured wing had been caused by a human, and not the currawongs and magpies as I originally thought. He had a habit of appearing from nowhere and buzzing us, succeeding in giving everyone a good fright if unprepared. I wondered if, maybe, he had flown at somebody and that person, thinking they were about to be attacked, had struck out at him.

I agonised for weeks about what to do; it was unfair to keep him locked-up, I didn't feel it was safe enough here at home, but I would now need to find somewhere where there were not so many houses and people around. Margaret (UFO's mother), came to my rescue with the suggestion of a fifty acre property owned by a couple she knew well. There were very few neighbours and Noel and Barbara loved birds, feeding quite a number of different species in their garden. The fact that a couple of drongos visited each year was encouraging and after quite a few sleepless nights trying to decide what would be in the bird's best interests, I made the heart-wrenching decision to relocate him.

Noel and Barbara didn't have an aviary to house the drongo and they generously offered to allow him to fly freely in a screened-off section of their large verandah. This allowed him to have a good view of his new surroundings and see the resident birds (and allow them to see him) before he was set free. A few days after his arrival one of the resident drongos began visiting him and as they seemed to be getting along, Barbara felt confident to release the confined bird. There wasn't any fighting with the wild birds and our drongo seemed to settle in quite well. He had flown into the house a couple of times, sitting on top of the television cabinet and throwing a few bits of paper around. However, most of the time he stayed outside, travelling around with the other birds. A week after his release he stopped visiting and we all felt sure that he had finally 'weaned' himself off human company. How wrong we were!

Belinda, another carer who lives in the general area where the drongo had been released, had a phone call from a couple with a "tame, black bird". They didn't know what sort of bird it was but wanted to know what to feed it and what size cage to build to house the bird. Fortunately, Belinda asked the couple to bring the bird to her for identification. They arrived with a drongo; captive in a laundry basket in which it had spent the last two days, being fed bread and water (real jailbird fare). I was so thankful for Belinda's gentle but firm manner in explaining to this couple that the bird was really a wild bird and it would be cruel (not to mention illegal) for them to keep it locked-up. They reluctantly handed the drongo over to her and Belinda set it free again on her own property.

The story filtered through the 'wildlife grapevine' to me and I suspected the bird was our drongo. I promptly rang Belinda and while I was talking to her, she mentioned that the drongo had just flown inside and was sitting on her head. "Quick," I said "Put the phone up to him and I'll say hello." As soon as he heard my voice he started chattering excitedly. He had so much to say and I'm sure he was telling me about the dreadful two days he had spent in the laundry basket! There was no longer any doubt in our minds that the bird was my drongo.

As tempted as I was to bring him home, I felt it was still in the bird's best interest to leave him where he was. Belinda has four children for him to play with and although she has neighbours, the area is not quite as built up as where I live. He comes and goes as he pleases and sometimes now disappears for weeks at a time. He has even flown back to Barbara and Noel's, immediately perching on the television cabinet and finding bits of paper to throw on the floor. Belinda is always relieved though, when he has been away for any length of time, to hear one of her children call out, "Mum, the drongo's back!"

Spangled Drongo

I fondly think back to the day not long after the drongo's first release when my parents-in-law had joined us for a lunchtime barbecue. The drongo had been entertaining us for hours with his antics. We had all laughed uproariously when Denis put the steak on the barbecue and the drongo flew down, perching near the hot plate, with a leaf held in his foot, as if to say "Here's my piece to cook!" He had sat on my mother-in-law's shoulder and at one stage, while he was sitting there, he had become a bit too boisterous and I attempted to shoo him away. He flopped forward, claws holding onto the fabric of her blouse and hung there, upside down, looking like a strange black brooch. He could be such a clown and like any performer he loved a crowd, the more the merrier. It had been a wonderful afternoon spent with our wild black pal and the day was drawing to a close when my father-in-law looked across at me. "You know, Peta" he said "Some people could count the number of friends they make in a lifetime on one hand. Over the years you have been so lucky to have had the friendship of so many of these birds. You must feel very fortunate?" *Yes, I certainly do, very fortunate indeed.*

ACKNOWLEDGEMENTS

We wish to thank the following people whose advice and support over the years has helped to make this book possible:

Jane Allen, Bev Birtles, Gerri Kluver, the late Lyn Irwin, Ailsa Watson, Phil and Rosemary Bender, Val Clark; Kay Collett from Applause Press; Veterinary Surgeons Angus Young, Michael Higgins and Graeme Lean and Associates; Gary Slack from Mooloolah Butchers; Russell and Bronwyn Wynn from Pet Affair; Jeff and Pauline Durston from Gull Cottage.

A special mention to Noel and Margaret Hewitt who allowed us to tell UFO's story, shared their computer and helped with the editing and proofreading.

To Kelly and Merryon Ryall and Anthony Ellison, we cannot thank you enough for your computer skills and to Don Ellison for his publishing experience.

A thank you to Rosemont, Hardys and McWilliams Wines for preserving our sanity!

To Denis and Don our heartfelt thanks for your wonderful support and for not complaining too much when a bird shares your home. Last but not least we thank our children Josh and Ryan, Kelly and Merryon. Although they had been scratched and bitten and also had to share their mothers' attention, they *still* helped with the raising of the birds. We dedicate this book to you.

STORIES & ILLUSTRATIONS BY:

Peta Boyce spent her childhood in Papua New Guinea where she developed a passion for wildlife at an early age. At different times animals kept in their home ranged from caterpillars and snails to a bat and sugar gliders.

Peta cares for injured and orphaned wildlife in her home in Mooloolah, Queensland and her love of caring for some of our smaller species of bird is reflected in her art. A self-taught artist working mainly in gouache, her paintings of robins, wrens, pardalotes and finches are extremely popular and her work is in private collections both in Australia and overseas. Peta has exhibited in a number of combined Art Exhibitions, had a successful solo exhibition and in 1998 had a joint exhibition with wildlife artist, Lyn Ellision, at Gull Cottage, in Springwood, Queensland. Peta is an Exhibiting Member of the Queensland Wildlife Art Society.

Lyn Ellison was inspired by a magical friendship with a white-backed magpie to change direction in her career from potter and sculptor to become a painter of Australian wildlife. Magpies are still her favourite subject but she has become passionate about all wild birds and animals and finds this a wonderful and exciting field to be involved in. From her home in the Coomera Valley, Queensland she has a wealth of subjects to base her paintings on; the ones she sees every day, living out their daily lives with patience, fortitude and humour. She also likes to travel far and wide in the Australian bush looking for inspiration and it was on one of these trips that she found Lucky, the wallaroo.

Lyn's original paintings are found in a number of galleries in Australia and she has produced 7 limited edition prints, many of which are sold out. Lyn had a successful solo exhibition and has won a number of prizes at wildlife exhibitions. At a joint exhibition with Peta Boyce, called "Feathers and Fur", the idea to produce illustrated books about the characters that came into their care evolved.